HALF DOLLARS

Classic Coins From the 1800s to Today

This book belongs to

_____

(write your name here)

Whitman Search & Save™

Half Dollars

© 2017 Whitman Publishing, LLC
1960 Chandalar Drive · Suite E · Pelham, AL 35124
ISBN: 0794844693
Printed in China

Correspondence concerning this book may be directed to Whitman Publishing, Attn: Search & Save, at the address above.

Whitman Publishing is a leading publisher of numismatic reference books, supplies, and storage and display products that help you build, appreciate, and share great collections. To browse our complete catalog, visit Whitman Publishing online at www.Whitman.com.

If you enjoy this Whitman Search & Save™ book, we invite you to start a new coin collection with *Search & Save: Abraham Lincoln Cents; Search & Save: Nickels; Search & Save: Old U.S. Dimes and Quarters*, and others!

You can join the American Numismatic Association (ANA), the nation's largest hobby group for coin collectors. The ANA Young Numismatists program is for collectors 5 to 17 years old. Collect coins, learn about numismatic collectibles, participate in auctions, and make friends with the YN program. Learn more at www.Whitman.com/ANA.

OCG™ COLLECTING GUIDE   WCG™   WHITMAN®

CONTENTS

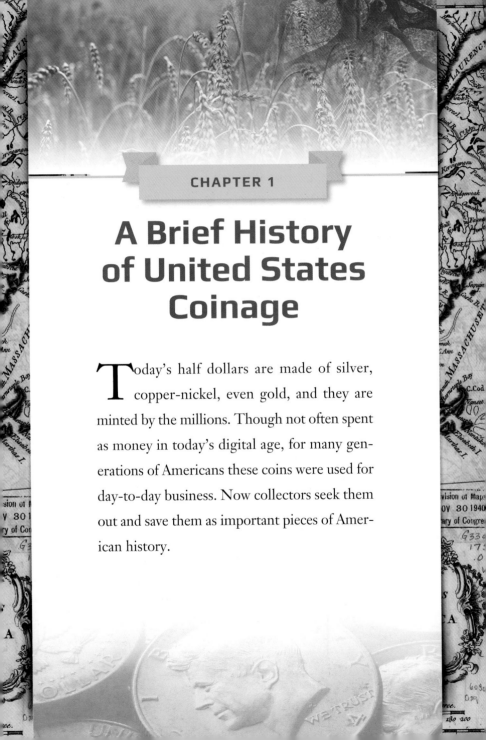

CHAPTER 1

A Brief History of United States Coinage

Today's half dollars are made of silver, copper-nickel, even gold, and they are minted by the millions. Though not often spent as money in today's digital age, for many generations of Americans these coins were used for day-to-day business. Now collectors seek them out and save them as important pieces of American history.

During America's colonial era of the 1600s and 1700s, people often used *barter* (trading) to pay for the things they needed. A farmer might trade part of his crop for a blacksmith's services, or a carpenter might bargain a fence repair for a pair of boots from the cobbler.

British colonists rarely used *specie* (silver or gold coins) as money amongst themselves, because Britain wanted its overseas territories to create wealth for *Britain*. British laws and policies encouraged the colonists to buy British products, discouraging them from making and selling their own finished goods. Gold and silver coins were paid to British merchants. Hard cash flowed from the New World *back* to the Old.

The colonists also weren't allowed to set up mints and strike their own coins. Only the kings and queens of England, and those they approved of, had that right.

IE COUNTRY EDITOR—PAYING THE YEARLY SUBSCRIPTION.—[DRAWN BY F. S. CHURCH.]

Americans have bartered—trading items instead of paying cash—for a long time. F.S. Church drew this illustration in 1874 depicting a man paying for the local-newspaper subscription with a chicken. The chicken traded for the newspaper is a form of barter.

The Revolutionary War started in 1775, and the American colonists declared their independence from Britain in 1776. A few state governments as well as individual Americans—private businessmen acting on their own—began to mint money that people could use in day-to-day transactions. Some of this money appeared in the form of official *coins* (legal tender), and some of it was *tokens* (not backed by the government). Some people even crafted counterfeit British halfpennies made to look like the real thing. During and after the war, there were few coins in circulation. Americans were so desperate for coins that they accepted whatever they could get their hands on, whether they were "real" or not. If it looked like a coin and was made of decent copper (or, even better, of silver), a shopkeeper would take it as payment, and his next customer would accept it in change.

Opposite page: During the American Revolution, Americans like these artillerymen and infantry officers would have spent Spanish, British, and other coins, plus paper bills, copper tokens, and other forms of money. There were no official United States coins yet—because there was no official "United States."

Copper coins from Massachusetts and Vermont.

A counterfeit British halfpenny minted in New York. Many of these fake coins were made to appear as if they'd been in circulation for a long time, encouraging their use by unsuspecting customers.

The U.S. Mint was headquartered in Philadelphia, the capital of the United States from 1790 to 1800.

The first half dollar was struck in 1794, to immediate popularity.

Finally, in 1791 Congress passed a law that authorized a national mint. This gave President George Washington the right to hire artists to design coins and buy machines to produce them. Washington made David Rittenhouse, a famous scientist, the first director of the Mint. In 1792 construction and renovation of buildings began in Philadelphia. The first U.S. coins made for the new Mint that year were silver half dismes (valued at five cents each), followed by dismes (ten cents) and half dollars (fifty cents) in 1794. The spelling of *disme* would later be changed to *dime*.

The first style of half dollars, called Flowing Hair, was minted in 1794 and 1795. Half dollars of the "Draped Bust" type were minted starting in 1796. Their design, of a long-haired woman symbolizing American Liberty, was created by Mint engraver Robert Scot and was similar to the design used on the half dime, dime, quarter, and silver dollar of that era. Not many of these early silver coins were made. Today they're rare and valuable.

Designed by Robert Scot, Draped Bust half dollars were minted from 1796 to 1807. Of those dated 1796 and 1797, only a few thousand are known today. (Shown enlarged.)

What Would a Half Dollar Buy?

1801

In 1801 the most expensive tavern dinners cost 50¢. Today, an expensive meal can cost more than $300!

1850

In 1850 it cost 50¢ to place an ad in a newspaper. Today advertising can cost hundreds, if not thousands, of dollars.

1860

It cost 50¢ to rent oxen to haul hay or other crops for short distances in 1860. In 2016 a truck rental could cost between $25 and $50.

1870s

A baseball ticket cost 50¢ during the 1870s. Today, a ticket to a ball game will cost $20 or more.

Oliver Hazard Perry's victory on Lake Erie during the War of 1812. Perry, master commandant of the USS *Lawrence*, won renown during the skirmish, which would be recognized as one of the largest naval battles of the entire war.

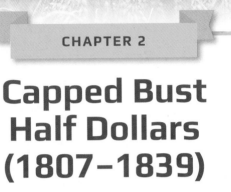

CHAPTER 2

Capped Bust Half Dollars (1807–1839)

In 1807 the Capped Bust design debuted. The motif of the woman with her elegant curls and cap were used in several variations on much of the coinage of the era. The new nation faced another battle with Great Britain in the War of 1812, then entered a time of national growth and enthusiasm. However, as the era of the Capped Bust coins neared its end in the 1830s, the United States was approaching a nationwide economic collapse.

Left: President Thomas Jefferson. *Right:* Meriwether Lewis and William Clark were sent by the president to explore and map the territory of the Louisiana Purchase in 1804. They were joined by a Shoshone Native American woman named Sacagawea, who served as their interpreter and guide.

In the election of 1800 Thomas Jefferson defeated John Adams for the presidency, becoming the third president of the fledgling nation. In 1803 the United States bought a huge amount of territory from France in the Louisiana Purchase, considered to be one of the most important acts of Jefferson's presidency. The Louisiana territory doubled the size of the United States (adding 827,000 square miles) and cost only $15 million. Included was land that would become the states of Oklahoma, Nebraska, Iowa, Kansas, and Missouri, and partial portions of Louisiana, Minnesota, Texas, Colorado, New Mexico, Wyoming, Montana, North Dakota, and South Dakota.

Meriwether Lewis and William Clark were tasked with exploring the new territory, and they left to do so in 1804, starting from St. Louis, Missouri. With them traveled a group of 33 people. They were later joined by a Shoshone Native American woman named Sacagawea, who served as their interpreter and guide. The group traversed thousands of miles from North Dakota to the Pacific Ocean, returning in 1806.

That same year the construction of the National Road, the first major highway in the United States, was authorized by President Jefferson. Called the "Cumberland Road" during its early stages, the new highway would replace old wagon and foot paths travelling between the Potomac and Ohio rivers, providing more secure transportation between Pennsylvania and Virginia. Construction of the road began in 1811 and continued until completion in 1837, reaching a total length of 620 miles.

Today Sacagawea's name is as well known as those of Lewis and Clark. In 2000 the U.S. Mint launched the Sacagawea dollar, featuring the famous Shoshone woman on the obverse.

In 1807 the Capped Bust half dollar debuted, with dimes and quarters of the same design following within a few years.

In 1807 John Reich, a German-born artist, started working full-time at the Philadelphia Mint as an engraver, after several years of contract work. He designed the new half dollar showing Miss Liberty, a symbol of American independence. In Reich's design she wears a cap with the word LIBERTY across its brim. This was one of the earliest federal coins to feature a denomination in its main design—50 C., for "50 cents." Before that, many U.S. coins either didn't show their values, or they were seen in tiny letters on the edge.

In 1809 Reich's half dollar Capped Bust design was introduced to the dime, and in 1815 to the quarter dollar. It would be used on all three coins into the late 1830s.

The 1809 dime bearing John Reich's Miss Liberty design, which debuted on the half dollar two years earlier.

Reich's Liberty design also was used on the quarter dollar.

At the beginning of the century, tensions were high between the newly formed United States, Britain, and France. Britain had been fighting the French emperor Napoleon Bonaparte since 1803, and soon the repercussions reached America. In 1807 Britain established trade restrictions to stop Americans from doing business with France. Worse, the Royal Navy began boarding American merchant ships and intercepting "deserters"—British sailors who had become naturalized

On October 25, 1812, the USS *United States* captured the HBM *Macedonian*. This was the first captured British warship to be brought into an American harbor.

American citizens. Britain did not recognize the sailors as Americans, and proceeded to seize them for forced service in the Royal Navy. The United States essentially considered this to be kidnapping. For these reasons and others, on June 18, 1812, Congress declared war against Britain. The two nations would battle on land and at sea from mid-1812 to late 1814.

After the conflict ended in 1815, America continued into a period of expansion that came to be known as the "Era of Good Feelings." The war had solidified patriotism in the United States, and many citizens put aside political differences. Investments in banking, transportation, and communications became priorities across the country. The Erie Canal was completed in 1825 and was the first passage between the Great Lakes and the eastern coast of the United States. Railroads spread across the states, bringing new industry. Better transportation led to increased westward expansion, and new states were added to the Union as more Americans travelled beyond the old frontier lands. The United States was in an era of prosperity and growth. As the Capped Bust coinage came to its end, however, economic troubles began to brew.

A worn Capped Bust half dollar of 1812.

The "Underground Railroad," a network of abolitionists who secretly helped many slaves escape to freedom, started as early as 1830. (Painting by Charles T. Webber.)

CHAPTER 3

Liberty Seated Half Dollars (1839–1891)

The era from the 1830s to the 1890s had its share of unrest in the United States, including the bloody years of the American Civil War. But these were also decades of growth, development, and promise. Throughout this period, the U.S. Mint made silver coins with a symbol of Miss Liberty seated with an American shield.

In 1837 an economic depression later known as the Panic of 1837 caused the failure of many banks across the country. Gold and silver coins became scarce as nervous citizens hoarded their hard cash. Nevertheless, the country recovered to survive through two ensuing wars—the Mexican-American War from 1846 to 1848 and the Civil War from 1861 to 1865. The years following saw many states, especially in the South, struggle to recover financially, but as the turn of the century approached America as a whole was entering a new industrial era of growth and prosperity.

Martin Van Buren, a key advisor to President Andrew Jackson, was ideally placed to run for the Democratic Party in the 1836 presidential election. He defeated several opponents in the Whig Party and took

Left: This dragoon (cavalryman) and infantry officer of 1847, at the time of the Mexican-American War, might have spent Liberty Seated coinage in day-to-day transactions. *Opposite page:* The Civil War–era (1863) engineer officer and infantry sergeant rarely would have spent Liberty Seated coins during the war, as gold, silver, and even copper coins were hoarded.

the presidency—but inherited a large problem. The economy was in a shambles, and when the Panic of 1837 left many in financial straits, his critics blamed the situation on the president. Certain newspapers of the era called him "Martin Van *Ruin*," and Congress resisted his attempts to regain prosperity. In 1840 Van Buren denied the admission of Texas into the Union, fearing to unbalance the number of free and slave states. As the economy continued to suffer, and as relations with Mexico and with Britain continued to be strained, Van Buren was voted out of office in 1840.

In 1844 Samuel Morse sent the first telegraph message, from Washington to Baltimore. It read, "What hath God wrought." The following year the Magnetic Telegraph Company was formed to erect telegraph lines from New York City down to Philadelphia, to Boston, Buffalo, and all the way to the Mississippi River. This progress was overshadowed by the outbreak of the Mexican-American War in 1846. The United States had annexed Texas, which led to border disputes and eventual bloodshed when Mexican troops crossed the Rio Grande and attacked American soldiers. By 1848 the war was over, with the United States victorious. Relations were understandably strained and hostile for a time, only normalizing slowly.

The decades following the war with Mexico saw a boom in industrialization. The railway spread across the nation, providing faster transportation and improving on the earlier miracle of the waterway canal. By 1856 Henry Bessemer had invented a process by which steel could be mass produced, allowing weaker and less sturdy cast iron and wrought iron to be replaced. New bridges and tracks were more structurally sound.

Industry was advancing, but America wasn't in the clear yet. Political and economic tensions were felt from North to South. Slavery was a dividing point between the nation's agricultural and industrial sectors.

Sir Henry Bessemer, an English inventor who developed the primary technique for making steel during the 1800s.

In 1857 the Ohio Life Insurance and Trust Company failed, causing thousands of businesses to collapse. That same year the SS *Central America* sank off of Charleston, dumping 30,000 pounds of gold into the ocean along with more than 420 passengers and crew. The loss of the gold contributed to the Panic of 1857, a financial depression mirroring the earlier Panic of 1837.

In 1859 Oregon was admitted as a state of the Union. The subject of slavery became more and more contentious: would future states allow slavery or outlaw it? After Abraham Lincoln was elected president, several Southern states broke away from the Union to form their own nation, the Confederate States of America.

Then—war. On April 12, 1861, open hostilities broke out between the North and the South, the Union and the Confederacy. Neighbor fought neighbor, and the long violent conflict would continue until the collapse of the rebel armies and government in the spring of 1865. The Union's victory was proclaimed on May 9 that year. American casualties from those four years totaled a higher number than the later deaths of World War I and World War II combined. And while the war saved the Union—and freed the slaves and abolished slavery in the United States—mending wounds was not easy. The Reconstruction Era lasted well into the 1870s.

The Civil War's Battle of Atlanta, July 1864, illustrated in a chromolithograph by Thulstrup de Thure, 1888.

Christian Gobrecht and sketches
of his Liberty Seated design.

Christian Gobrecht began working for the Mint as early as 1823, when Robert Scot, the chief engraver at the time, passed away. Originally Gobrecht's appointment was temporary, but his employment with the Mint became permanent when William Kneass was hired as chief engraver in 1824. Gobrecht specialized in pattern and die work, and as early as 1836 his Liberty Seated design (based on sketches by Thomas Sully and Titian Peale) was used on dollar coins. It appeared on the half dime and the dime in 1837, and in 1838 on the quarter dollar. The half dollar followed suit in 1839.

In 1840 Gobrecht was appointed the chief engraver of the Mint. And though he passed away in 1844, his design would continue on for decades afterward.

The Liberty Seated half dollar design was struck continuously from 1839 to 1891, never missing a year.

One variety of Liberty Seated half dollar has arrows pointing from the date, and rays around the eagle—details lacking on the first design of 1839 to 1853. There would be five varieties over the years, with minor design differences.

"Passage of the Delaware" by Thomas Sully.

Inset: Thomas Sully and Titian Peale were both American artists whose work was used on U.S. coinage.

The Liberty Seated design was used on several denominations of U.S. coins. The general style is the same for all, though with small alterations. The figure of Liberty sits in a flowing dress upon a rock, holding her iconic Liberty pole and Phrygian cap. The cap-and-pole is a symbol of freedom dating back to ancient Greece and Rome. A *pileus* (cap) was an identifier for a freed slave. The cap was placed atop the pole following the assassination of Julius Caesar in 44 BCE, symbolizing the freedom of the Roman people from Caesar's tyrannous rule. The symbol also became significant to rebelling colonists during the American Revolution.

In Liberty's right hand is a striped shield, with a diagonal banner bearing the word LIBERTY streaming across its face. The shield shows American preparedness to defend freedom.

A silver dollar (1836) with the Liberty Seated design.

"The Three Wise Men," each wearing a Phrygian cap as they present gifts to Mary and Jesus.

On February 3, 1870, the United States ratified the 15th Amendment, prohibiting any citizen from being denied the right to vote based on race, color, or "previous condition of servitude." The following years brought civil unrest as members of the Ku Klux Klan were tried and convicted in federal courts, as African-American politicians were elected to seats in Congress, and as Jim Crow laws were enacted in Tennessee, prompting the Civil Rights Act of 1875. This act put into federal law the guarantee of equal treatment to black Americans in terms of public accommodations, transportation, and jury service.

The 1880s brought an economic and industrial boom. Railroads continued to improve. The "skyscraper" was invented with the erection of buildings 10 to 20 floors high, much taller than earlier construction. The Brooklyn Bridge was opened in 1883, and in 1885 the Washington Monument was completed. More states were admitted to the Union, and the country's population exceeded 50 million. As this growth was taking place, civil rights in America struggled: there were lynchings of black Americans in the South, and in 1883 the policy of segregation (separation of white and black people) was legalized as the Civil Rights Act of 1875 was deemed unconstitutional. With growth and turmoil, America entered the last decade of the century.

A Liberty Seated dime.

Opposite page: At the base of the partially completed Washington Monument the Army's chief of engineers, Lieutenant Colonel Thomas Casey, discusses the construction with a civilian contractor and two junior engineer officers. *Overset:* The Liberty Seated design on coins of the era: a tiny half dime and a much larger half dollar.

Before 1890, the natural wonders of California's Yosemite Valley and its surroundings, including Tenaya Lake, seen here, were not protected as national parklands.

On October 1, 1890, Congress designated Yosemite a national park. The following year Carnegie Hall opened in New York City. In 1892 Grover Cleveland was elected president, becoming the first (and, so far, only) president to serve two terms non-consecutively.

Just as the 1893 World's Columbian Exposition was opening in Chicago, another economic panic pushed the United States into a severe depression, prompting industrial workers to strike. Coxey's Army, made up of unemployed workers led by Ohio businessman Jacob Coxey, marched on Washington, D.C., to lobby the government to create more jobs. In an attempt to honor laborers and appease the angry workforce, Congress created the national holiday of Labor Day in 1894. Two years later the United States participated in the first modern Olympic Games, held in Athens, Greece; U.S. athletes won the most gold medals. William McKinley was elected president. By the end of the decade the Klondike Gold Rush had begun in Alaska, and the United States declared war on Spain. A new decade was beginning, and with it would come new coins. Liberty Seated was on her way out.

Laborers march on Washington, D.C., to protest widespread unemployment.

PRICE 25 CE

LIFE

The cover of *Life* magazine, No. 908, April 7, 1900.

EASTER

1900

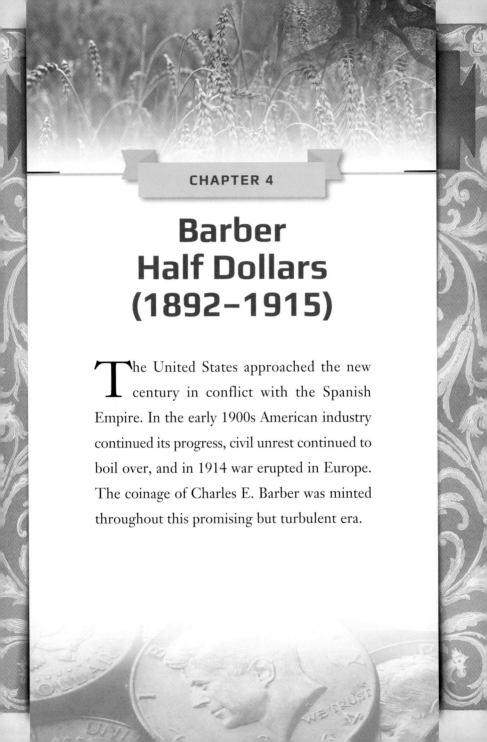

CHAPTER 4

Barber Half Dollars (1892–1915)

The United States approached the new century in conflict with the Spanish Empire. In the early 1900s American industry continued its progress, civil unrest continued to boil over, and in 1914 war erupted in Europe. The coinage of Charles E. Barber was minted throughout this promising but turbulent era.

In 1896 William McKinley was elected as president. His first term saw rapid growth in the economy, as well as new rules to protect factory workers and manufacturers.

War broke out between the United States and Spain in 1898, brought on by American ambitions and escalating disputes between the two countries. The conflict was one-sided, with the United States easily beating the aging Spanish Empire. Hostilities lasted only three months, three weeks, and two days. The concluding 1898 Treaty of Paris liberated Cuba and made Puerto Rico, Guam, and the Philippine Islands territories of the United States.

The U.S. population rose above 75 million in 1900, stretching across the states from the East to the West. In 1901 the nation mourned after the assassination of President McKinley. Vice President Theodore Roosevelt stepped into his place and became a leader known for reform in his own right. Roosevelt established newly protected national parks and forests during his presidency with the intention of preserving the country's natural resources.

The World's Fair was held in St. Louis in 1904. Construction of the Panama Canal began under President Roosevelt's watch, and in 1906 he was awarded the Nobel Peace Prize for negotiating several international peace treaties.

In 1908 the Federal Bureau of Investigation was established, and in 1909 the Lincoln cent (the "penny" everyone in America knows) saw its debut. That year William Howard Taft became the 27th president of the United States.

Opposite page: One of the last photographs taken of President William McKinley alive, while ascending the steps of the Temple of Music, a concert hall and auditorium in Buffalo, New York. McKinley was shot by an anarchist shortly after the photo was taken, on September 6, 1901. He died a few days later. Congress then put the Secret Service in official charge of protecting the president.

Charles E. Barber, chief engraver of the U.S. Mint (second from left, bottom row), in a photograph of Mint staff. *Opposite page:* Barber's half dollar.

Chief engraver Charles E. Barber was the designer behind the Liberty Head motif that is found on not only the half dollar but also on similarly designed dimes and quarters of the late 1800s and early 1900s. The coin shows Miss Liberty in profile, wearing a cap and a crown of fronds similar to designs found on French coins of the era. The Barber half dollar was struck every year from 1892 to 1915.

In 1892 there were four mints operating in the United States, and the Barber half dollar was produced at three of them: Philadelphia, New Orleans, and San Francisco. (The Carson City Mint produced only silver dollars that year.) Mintmarks identifying the New Orleans and San Francisco production facilities are seen as small letters (an "O" or an "S") located beneath the eagle on the reverse. In addition, Barber's initial "B" appears at the base of Miss Liberty's neck.

For his 1892 design, Chief Engraver Barber was influenced artisti-
cally by French coinage of the 1800s. Similar to America's Miss Liberty,
Marianne serves as one of France's national symbols. She is an allegory
of freedom and reason, a portrayal of the goddess Liberty. Marianne
became popular in France during the French Revolution of 1789, when
Liberty was viewed as leading the people out from under the rule of
the oppressive monarchy. She is often seen wearing the Phrygian cap,
symbol of freedom.

Above: "Liberty Leading the People," by Eugène Delacroix, 1830. *Opposite page:* "Paris in the
Phrygian Cap," painted by Antoni Brodowski in 1812.

Marianne on three French coin designs of the 1870s to early 1900s, similar to Miss Liberty on Charles Barber's U.S. silver coinage (also pictured).

Turn-of-the-century fashion, as published in New York.

The second decade in the new century would forever be known as one rife with conflict and tragedy. In 1912 the RMS *Titanic*, a British passenger liner carrying more than 2,000 passengers and crew, sank in the North Atlantic Ocean. More than 1,500 of those on board died, making the disaster one of the deadliest ever during peacetime. That same year former president Theodore Roosevelt was campaigning for a third term when he was shot by an unemployed saloonkeeper. Roosevelt survived the attack and even continued on his way to a scheduled speech, where he unbuttoned his bloodstained vest and told the crowd, "It takes more than that to kill a bull moose!"

On July 28, 1914, war broke out in Europe—a global conflict that would become known as the Great War for generations after.

L'INGORDO

THE HIM OF HATE

British and French cartoonists often drew the German emperor, Wilhelm II, as an ogre hungry for world domination, and the cause of the Great War. In reality the conflict was far bigger and more complex than any single European ruler.

The roots of World War I were planted many years before the first bullets were fired in 1914. The visible cause of the conflict was the assassination of Archduke Franz Ferdinand of Austria, which created a diplomatic crisis that spread wildly out of control. In a matter of weeks the major nations of Europe were at war, dividing into the Allied Powers (France, the British Empire, Russia, Italy, Romania, and others) and the Central Powers (Germany, Austria-Hungary, the Ottoman Empire, and others). The United States would officially associate with the Allies in 1917.

4 CYL. MODEL T FORD, 1908

© The GROGAN PHOTO COMPANY Danville, Ill.

In 1908 the Ford Motor Company produced the Model T, which would remain in production until 1927. In 1913 Henry Ford invented the concept for the modern assembly line, which took manufacturing and production levels to an all-new high.

The new technology and military strategies of the age (including trench warfare, poison gas, airplanes, tanks, long-range artillery, and submarines) made war very different than it ever had been before. More than 70 million soldiers and military personnel were mobilized. Of these, 9 million combatants were killed in addition to 7 million civilians.

By the time the conflict officially ended in November 1918, the social landscape of the world was changed. The political strength of women had become more evident as many joined the workforce and took business positions normally held by men (now soldiers drafted into the war effort). Many of Europe's kings lost their thrones and were replaced by democratic or socialist leaders. The British Empire began to decline, with some of its colonies seeking independence. The Ottoman Empire collapsed completely, as did the empires of Austria-Hungary and Russia. Europe's economies were in shambles, and the United States emerged as the wealthy and powerful banker to the world. In *American Gold and Silver: U.S. Mint Collector and Investor Coins and Medals, Bicentennial to Date,* Dennis Tucker describes the end of the gold standard and the rise of inflation after the Great War, noting that "after the war, half of the world's gold was held by the United States."

ALLENTOWN DEMO[C]

TH YEAR — ALLENTOWN, PA., TUESDAY MORNING, NOVEMBER 12, 1918

WHOLE NATION JUBILANTLY CELE[BRATES] VICTORIOUS ENDING OF THE W[AR]

"KNOCKOUT" IS [S]ENT ACROSS BY [A]MERICAN GUNS

[Ya]nkee Artillery Along 75 Mile Front Blazes Away in Final Salvo —"The Kaisers Knockout."

[By T]he Universal Service.—
[WI]TH THE AMERICAN FIRST [ARM]Y, Nov. 11.—On the dot of 11 [o'clock] this morning the great war [passe]d into history.

American batteries along a 75 [mile] front were blazing salvoes [christ]ened "the kaiser's knockout."

[The] army was notified that the ar[mistic]e was signed at 5.45 o'clock a. [m. H]eadquarters sent out orders by [wirele]ss and telephone that hostili[ties w]ere to cease at 10.55 a. m. on the [Americ]an side, and at 11 a. m. on the [Germ]an side, there being five min[utes] difference between German and [Frenc]h time on the fronts. This re[sulted] in the cessation of fighting at [the s]ame instant on both sides.

It is quite likely that many [men] in the front line are not yet in[forme]d, owing to the great difficulty [of ma]intaining good communications [with] the rear guard during a rapid [advan]ce such as has marked the last [few d]ays.

[It is] possible some clashes occurred [after] the armistice went into effect. [It i]s known that the German dele[gates] were anxious for the earliest [possib]le suspension of hostilities after [the si]gning of the document.

[Grea]t fleets of airplanes dropped [messag]es to the front line troops [inform]ing them of the suspension of [hostili]ties.

[As t]he echoes of the final cannons [were] dying on the Scarpe hills [and c]rests, the dough boys waltzed, [two-s]tepped and threw up their [hats a]nd fired revolvers and rifles in [the air]. They set off flares and made [a regul]ar Fourth of July celebration [of the] event.

[Old] Glory was unfurled, the black[ened t]rees serving as flag-poles. There [were s]peeches and cheers and unend[ing sh]outing.

["Fini]s la guerre" was the general [cry, b]orrowed from the French.

[Need]less to say the first thought [of Ame]rica's fighting boys belonged [to thei]r mothers, wives, sisters and [sweethe]arts. The question "wonder [what th]e folks back home are think[ing an]d doing back home?" was in all [minds] and upon all lips.

[The] civilians tonight gave vent to [their f]eelings in the rear zones. The [moment]ous event has stirred the [hearts] of all men, women and child[ren to] their depths. The scenes of [rejoici]ng are difficult to scribe. Every [day fo]r several days the news of [the sig]ning of the armistice had been [expecte]d. The last Sunday in the great [war wa]s marked by curious contrasts [of men] fighting in the front lines, the [men in] the rear relaxing with antic-

MARSHAL FOCH'S ORDER DIRECTING FIGHTING TO STOP

Allied Troops Not to Go Beyond Line Reached Today Until Further Orders

MESSAGE SENT BY GERMAN DELEGATES

Marshal Foch's Order Sent Immediately After Signing of Armistice

PARIS, Nov. 11.—Here is the order which Marshal Foch sent to all commanders on the west front immediately after the armistice was signed.

"Hostilities will cease on the whole front as from Nov. 11 at 11 o'clock, French time. The allied troops will not, until further order, go beyond the line reached on that day and on that hour."

(Signed) "Marshal Foch."

The following message was sent by wireless by the German armistice plenipotentiaries:

"To the German high command, to be communicated to all authorities interested:

"Radio received, Armistice was signed at 5 o'clock in the morning, French time. It comes into force at 11 o'clock in the morning, French time. Delay for evacuation prolonged by 24 hours for the left bank of the Rhine, making 31 days in all. Modifications of the text compared with that brought by Helldorf will be transmitted by radio."

(Signed) "Erzberger."

STOCK EXCHANGES CLOSE FOR THE DAY

Members Everywhere Wanted to Participate in Peace Celebration

By The Universal Service.—
NEW YORK, Nov. 11.—Stock and other exchanges througout the United States closed today to allow their members to participate in the peace celebration.

The New York stock exchange led in declaring a holiday, and the others quickly followed its example. Among the important exchanges which closed were the New York produce exchange, the New York cotton exchange, the New York Curb Market, the Chicago Stock Exchange and Board of Trade, the New York Consolidated Stock Exchange, the New York Metal Market, the Boston Stock Exchange, the Pittsburgh Stock Exchange and the Philadelphia Stock Exchange. Banks remained open, as only a proclamation by the governor announcing a legal holiday would overcome the legal obstacle.

ARMISTICE TERMS LEAVE GERMANY POWERLESS TO RESUME HOSTILITIES

WASHINGTON, Nov. 11—"The war thus comes to an end."

At exactly 1.21 o'clock this afternoon President Wilson uttered these words in the house of representatives at the joint session

It was his official announcement of the ending of the war. It was his declaration to the congress that had authorized the call to arms that the aim, hopes and aspirations of the enemies of militarism had been achieved. Pandemonium broke loose. Senators and representatives leaped to their feet with a mighty shout of enthusiasm. They clapped their hands and cheered the president as they had never done before. The whole congress, Democrats and Republicans alike, was united in the outburst of applause and approval.

Up beneath the rostrum directly below the stand whereon the president waited, sat the venerable justices of the supreme court with Chief Justice White in the center. They, too, arose and applauded with vigor.

At the left of the president, in the corner of the great hall sat the diplomatic corps and the members of the president's cabinet, as the sentence's full portent, though consisting only of seven words, fell from the president's lips they were up with the rest of them cheering and clapping their hands.

And the galleries, where applause is strictly forbidden while the house is in session, threw the rules to the winds as the waves of applause sweeping upward from the floor of the chamber were sent back in a tremendous echo.

Mrs. Wilson was seated in the executive gallery with other members of the president's party.

The demonstration lasted several minutes. It was brought to a close only because those who were listening were eager to hear what the president had to say of the further settlement that is to come and of the final triumph of peace.

The scenes in the house during the delivery of the president's mes[sage] was in sharp contrast to the s[cenes in] the same hall months ago w[hen the] president announced that [war with] Germany was unavoidable [...] the days of sober thou[ght ...] and representatives w[ho heard the] president that day we[re ...] thoughtful on that day [...] number were even op[posed] into it and upon thei[r faces were] frowns that betrayed th[...]al.

But today all were in [...] were glad—glad not that th[e war was] over, but that it had been won. There was no lack of unity among them. There was no chance of discord over the wonderful message that the president came to give them. The whole atmosphere breathed of triumph and of victorious accomplishment which carried a quickening of the blood to everybody in the house.

Chief Justice White, seated immediately below the president, never appeared more amiable as he looked up into the president's face, drank in the words that spells the downfall of the German empire. Once near the beginning of the president's address, when the president announced that the German authorities had signed the armistice, the chief justice shouted "bravo" and started the first round of applause.

In addressing congress the president said:

"Gentlemen of the congress:

"In these anxious times of rapid and stupendous changes it will in some degree lighten my sense of responsibility to perform in person the duty of communicating to you some of the large circumstances of the situation with which it is necessary to deal. The German authorities who have at the invitation of the supreme war council, been in communication with Marshal Foch have accepted and signed the terms of armistice which he was authorized and instructed to communicate to them. These terms are as follows:

"I—Military clauses on western front.

"1—Cessation of operations by land, and in the air six hours after the signature of the armistice.

"2—Immediate evacuation of invaded countries: Belgium, France, Alsace-Lorraine, Luxemberg, ordered as to be completed within 14 days from the signature of the armistice. German troops which have not left the above mentioned territories within the period fixed, will become prisoners of war. Occupation by the Allied and United States forces jointly will keep pace with evacuation in these areas. All movements of evacuation and occupation will be regulated in accordance with a note annexed to the stated terms.

"3—Repatriation beginning at once and to be completed within fourteen days of all inhabitants of the countries above mentioned, including hostages and persons under trial or convicted.

"4—Surrender in good condition by the German armies of the following equipment: Five thousand guns (two [thousand five hund]red heavy, two [thousand five hundred] field), 30,000 [machine guns, 3,000 minen]werfer [...] and mine[...] [...] [...]elanes [...] [...]the 7th [...]. The [...] and [...]nce [...]n.

[...] heads at these points in 30 kilometer radius on the right bank and by garrisons, similarly holding the strategic points of the regions. A neutral zone shall be reserved on the right of the Rhine between the stream and a line drawn parallel to it forty kilometers to the east from the frontier of Holland to the parallel of Gernsheim and as far as practicable, a distance of thirty kilometers from the east of stream from this parallel upon Swiss frontier. Evacuation by the enemy of the Rhinelands shall be so ordered as to be completed within a further period of eleven days, in all nineteen days after the signature of the armistice. All movements of regulated according to the note annexed.

"6—In all territory evacuated by the enemy there shall be no evacuation of inhabitants; no damage or harm shall be done to the persons or property of the inhabitants; no destruction of any kind to be committed. Military establishments of all kinds shall be delivered intact, as well as military stores of food, munitions, equipment not removed during the periods fixed for evacuation. Stores of food of all kinds for the civil population, etc., shall be left in situ. Industrial establishments shall not be impaired in any way and their personnel shall not be moved. Roads and means of communication of every kind, railroads, waterways, main roads, bridges, telegraphs, telephones shall be in no manner impaired.

"7—All civil and military personnel at present employed on them shall remain. Five thousand locomotives, 50,000 wagons and 10,000 motor lorries in good working order, with all necessary spare parts and fittings shall be delivered to the associated powers within the period fixed for the evacuation of Belgium and Luxemburg. The railways of Alsace-Lorraine shall be handed over within the same period, together with all pre-war personnel and material. Further material necessary for the working of railways in the country on the left bank of the Rhine shall be kept in situ. All stores of coal and material for the upkeep of permanent ways, signals and repair shops left entire in situ, and kept in an efficient state by Germany during the whole period of armistice. All barges taken from the Allies shall be restored to them.

(Note appended regulates the details).

"8—German command shall be responsible for revealing all mines or delay acting fuses disposed on territory evacuated by the German troops and shall assist in their discovery and destruction. The Germans command shall so reveal all destructive measures that may have been taken (such as poisoning or polluting of springs, wells, etc.) under penalty of reprisals.

"9—The right of requisition shall be exercised by the Allied and the United States armies in all occupied territory. The upkeep of the troops of occupation in the Rhine land (excluding Alsace-Lorraine) shall be charged to the German government.

"10—An immediate repatriation without reciprocity, accor[ding to de]tailed conditions which [...] of all Allied and U[nited States pris]oners of war. Th[...] the United State[s ...] pose of these [...]

"11—Sick [and wounded who cannot] be removed [...] will be ca[red for by German person]nel who w[ill be left on the spot with] the medic[al material required].

"12—Di[...] [...]era fro[...]

"12—All German troops at present in any territory which before the war belonged to Russia, Rumania or Turkey shall withdraw within the frontiers of Germany as they existed on August 1st, 1914.

"13—Evacuation by German troops to begin at once and all German instructors, prisoners and civilian as well as military agents, now on the territory of Russia (as defined before 1914) to be recalled.

"14—German troops to cease at once all requisitions and seizures and any other undertakings with a view to obtaining supplies intended for Germany in Rumania and Russia (as defined on August 1, 1914).

"15—Abandonment of the treaties of Bucharest and Brest Litovsk and of the supplementary treaties.

"16—The Allies shall have free access to the territories evacuated by the Germans on their eastern front or either through Danzig or by the Vistula in order to convoy supplies to the populations of those territories or for any other purpose.

"III.—Clause concerning East Africa:

"17—Unconditional capitulation of all German forces operating in East Africa within one month.

"18—Repatriation without reciprocity, within a maximum period of one month, in accordance with detailed conditions hereafter to be fixed, of all civilians interned or deported who may be citizens of other Allied or associated states than those mentioned in clause three, paragraph nineteen, with the reservation that any future claims and demands of the Allies and the United States of America remain unaffected.

"19—The following financial conditions are required: Reparation for damage done. While such armistice lasts no public securities shall be removed by the enemy which can serve as a pledge to the Allies for the recovery or reparation for war losses. Immediate restitution of the cash deposit, in the National Bank of Belgium, and in general immediate return of all documents, specie, stocks, shares, paper money together with plant for the issue thereof, touching public or private interests in the invaded countries. Restitution of the Russian and Rumanian gold yielded to Germany or taken by that power. This gold to be delivered in trust to the Allies until the signature of peace.

"20—Immediate cessation of all hostilities at sea and definite information to be given as to the location and movements of all German ships. Notification to be given to neutrals that freedom of navigation in all territorial waters is given to the naval and mercantile marines of the Allied and associated powers, all questions of neutrality being waived.

"21—All naval and mercantile marine prisoners of war of the Allied and associated Powers in German hands to be returned without reciprocity.

"22—Surrender to the Allies and the United States of America of one hundred and sixty German submarines (including all submarine cruisers and [mine] laying submarines), with their [complete a]rmament and equipment in [ports which] will be specified by the [Allies and U]nited States of Ameri[ca. All sub]marines to be paid off [...] [dis]armed and placed [under the supervisi]on of the Allied [and Unite]d States of Am[erica].

[...] [G]erman surface [warships] designated by [the Allies and Un]ited States of [...] Twelve.)

[...] BATTLESHIP [SUN]K ON SATURDAY

[British] Admiralty Makes An[noun]cement of Torpedoing of Britannia

[LOND]ON, Nov. 11.—The admiralty [announc]es that the H. M. S. Britania [was to]rpedoed and sunk at the [western] entrance of the strait of [Gibralt]ar on Saturday Nov. 9.

[The] Britania was a battle ship of [1]7,000 tons. She was built in [...]r normal complement was 780 [officers] and men. Only a few were

[...]D MARSHAL HAIG'S [B]RIEF NIGHT REPORT

[LOND]ON, Nov. 11—10.21 p. m.—[Hostiliti]es were suspended this [morning], says tonight's report from [Field M]arshal Haig.

["The B]ritish line runs from the Bel[gian-Fren]ch frontier to the east of Av[esnes, to] Avemount, to Givry, to four [miles ea]st of Mons, to Chievres, to [Lessines,] to Grammont."

[...]CYCLE DAMAGED WHEN STRUCK BY AUTO

NUMERAL ELEVEN AND END OF WAR

Fighting Stopped at 11th Hour of the 11th Day of 11th Month of Year

WASHINGTON, Nov. 11.—Although the great war did not end in accordance with the numerous prophecies of seers and star gazers, the great finale was cryptic to this extent:

Hostilities closed on the eleventh day of the eleventh month of the year, and at the eleventh hour of that day, and in addition the eleventh hour was truly Germany's eleventh hour, as the armistice terms show.

DAILY BULLETIN OF THE ALLENTOWN HOSPITAL

Admissions—James Kunkle, 451 Allen St., Mrs. Brooke Reichenbach, 524 North 6th St., Jacob Widonger, 751 North 9th St., Chas. Fatzer, Lehigh Church, George Frantz, 125 So. Law St., Dorothy Keller, 409 E. Walnut St., Mrs. Sadie Seiders, 257 So. Penn St., William Brong, 323 E. Union St., Edna Walters, city, Christine Smith, Walnut St., Edwin Erb, 102 North 8th.

Discharged—Mrs. Anna Moll, 7st St., Mrs. Rebecca Emery, 962 Chew St., Mrs. Lottie Reed, 202 Hickory St., Mrs. Traugh, 1026 Chew St., Miss Annie

SLATINGTON HAS BIG DEMONSTRATIO[N]

In celebration of the ending of the great world war, Slatington held the largest parade in its history last evening, with fully 5000 people from the borough and surrounding territory in line. The line of march formed at Slatedale shortly before 7 o'clock and wended its way into Slatington, where the local organizations and in fact almost everybody in the town joined in, with Burgess Harry Muschlitz as marshal. The Slatington Band, Slatedale Band and Knights of Freindship Drum Corps supplied the music. Many beautiful floats were in line, and among other things there were several hundred decorated automobiles from the surrounding country.

ST. PAUL'S REFORMED OPENED WHEN NEWS CAME

At four o'clock yesterday morning St. Paul's Reformed church, Fourteenth Ward, Rev. E. Elmer Sensenig, pastor, was opened for admission of the members and friends who wished to praise and worship for the good news which the nation had received in

[...] IS [...] TO U. S.

Arthur [...] a son of Mr. and Mrs. Peter A. Beisel of 136 North Church St., an expert cable splicer with the American Expeditionary forces has been invalided home to recuperate from an attack of rheumatism. Mr. Beisel who was a member of the signal corps arrived at Staten Island late last week and on Sunday telephoned to his father that he was in this country to regain his health and could be seen at the New York camp for a short time previous to his being sent to a health resort in the middle west. Two weeks after his enlistment he was across seas.

The senior Beisel and his son's wife left yesterday morning for Staten Island.

Before enlisting more than a year ago Mr. Beisel was employed by the Bell Telephone company in its cable department and was one of the most experienced men in the company's employ in this city. He is 30 years of age and previous to his enlistment was subject to attacks of his present

CARDI[NAL ...] FO[...]

BALTIM[ORE ...] Gibbons bro[...] today during [...] celebration he[re ...] from a window [...] waved an American [flag ...] was passing.

STRUCK BY AUTOMOBILE

Claude Nothstein, a fireman on the Lehigh Valley road, was run down by an automobile at 11 o'clock last night at 5th and Hamilton Sts., and removed to his boarding house 440 North Jordan St. in the machine. He suffered nothing more than a few cuts and bruises and a general shaking up.

INJURIED DURING CELEBRATION

Suffering from concussion of the brain, received yesterday afternoon in an accident during the peace demonstration, William Brong, of 323 Union St., was admitted to the Allentown hospital. Reports last evening were

[...]SCRIPTION

[...]—An official [order has be]en issued stopp[ing all re]cruiting through[...]. All calling up [...]led.

[FULTON CO]UNTY DRAFTEES [ARR]IVE AT CAMP CRANE

Fifty selected men who left their respective communities in Fulton county yesterday morning before instructions were received to abandon entrainment of drafted men, arrived in this city last evening at 7.45 o'clock for Camp Crane.

MORE RULERS GO.

COPENHAGEN, Nov. 11—The grand duke of Oldenburg has been dethroned and the Grand Duke of Mecklenberg Has Schwerin has abdicated, according to despatches from Hamburg.

The Hamburg Nachrichten, which reports the abdication of the Grand Duke, says that a government for Mecklenburg has been formed by a Workers and Sailors' Council

CHAPTER 5

Liberty Walking Half Dollars (1916–1947)

The silver half dollar of 1916 to 1947 debuted the same year as a new dime and quarter dollar. Today all three coins are widely collected as American classics. The era of the Liberty Walking half dollar spanned from the Great War through the Roaring Twenties, the Great Depression, and World War II.

The United States enjoyed economic prosperity after the Great War, and the following decade came to be known as the Roaring Twenties. Social, artistic, and cultural innovation bloomed, and Americans rushed to buy automobiles, telephones, home appliances, and luxuries—often on credit. Motion pictures and radio shows entertained the nation, and electricity was brought into more and more communities. Commercial, passenger, and freight aviation took off. Sports heroes and movie stars became media-powered celebrities. The U.S. population exceeded 100 million in 1920.

Jazz and dancing became popular pastimes as Americans threw off the malaise of the war. The delight in modern-day luxuries was widespread, earning social criticism as well as becoming a subject for tabloids and gossip. Not everyone was satisfied with the new enthusiasm of the age, though—some artists and authors such as Ernest Hemingway, Gertrude Stein, and F. Scott Fitzgerald expressed their resentment toward materialism.

This era also saw the introduction of so-called flapper girls, trendy young women who drank, smoked, danced, wore short hair and short dresses, and were confident and bold.

On August 18, 1920, the 19th amendment to the Constitution was ratified. This forced all the states to allow American women to vote. Before the amendment, 21 of the 48 states still kept them from the polls. That November, more than 8 million women voted in elections for the first time.

The exuberant prosperity was, sadly, not to last—in 1929 the stock market crashed, and the nation (along with the rest of the world) entered a period of poverty and unemployment known as the Great Depression. Meanwhile, in Europe, discontent festered in Germany over the peace treaty of Versailles, which forced the Germans to publicly accept guilt "for causing all the loss and damage" of the war and required them to pay huge reparations (financial compensation equal to $442 billion in 2016 dollars), which caused high inflation and poverty. In 1939, while America was still finding its feet economically, Germany invaded Poland, and the Second World War began. It would continue for six grueling years.

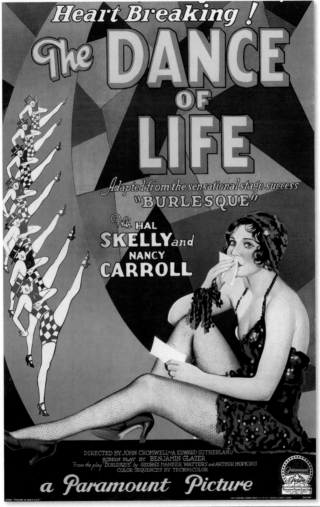

In 1929 Paramount released "The Dance of Life," a film that captured the energy of the Jazz Age.

Adolph A. Weinman was the artist behind the Liberty Walking half dollar.

Adolph A. Weinman, the artist who created the "Mercury" (Winged Liberty Head) dime of 1916, also designed the Liberty Walking half dollar. He was a German-born medalist and architectural sculptor, well known for the bronze reproductions of his larger statues and artistic works.

The obverse of the half dollar features a beautiful Miss Liberty, draped in a neoclassical gown as she strides toward the sun. Weinman's monogram can be seen beneath the tips of the eagle's wings on the reverse.

The coin was struck intermittently from 1916 to 1947, so there are some missing dates (1922, 1924, 1925, 1926, 1930, 1931, and 1932). In 1986 the Liberty Walking design was the basis of the American Silver Eagle one-ounce bullion coin, which has been struck every year since.

Weinman was a sculptor as well as a designer. His statue *The Setting Sun* was featured on this cover of *Sunset, The Pacific Monthly* magazine.

Weinman's *The Voice of Reason*, displayed at the Environmental Protection Agency, Ronald Reagan Building, Washington, D.C.

The Liberty Walking half dollar.

Adolph Weinman's design later was used on the American Silver Eagle one-ounce bullion coin.

Audrey Marie Munson was an artists' model and film actress in America during the 1900s. She was considered to be "America's First Supermodel" and was variously called "Miss Manhattan," "American Venus," the "Panama-Pacific Girl," and the "Exposition Girl." The last two nicknames came from her posing for the majority of statues created for the Panama-Pacific International Exposition of 1915. She was also the model or inspiration for more than a dozen statues in New York City. Adolph Weinman hired her as a model for some of his sculptures, including *The Setting Sun* (seen page 50). She was also a model for his 1916 coinage designs.

Audrey Munson posed for both the Liberty Walking half dollar and the "Mercury" or Winged Liberty Head dime, designed by Adolph Weinman.

People gathering outside of the New York Stock Exchange after the Great Crash of 1929.

Many factors led to the economic crash at the end of the Roaring Twenties. Individuals were consuming too much, buying expensive goods, often on installment plans and with shaky credit. Businesses reinvested their record-setting profits to the point of creating a financial bubble. Banks had no guarantees in place to protect account holders, which encouraged panics (people trying to quickly withdraw all or most of their cash) when markets went down. Banks also loaned money recklessly through the 1920s, as speculators borrowed to invest in the hot stock market. The house of cards toppled down on October 29, 1929, "Black Tuesday." On that day some 16 million stocks were traded and the market crashed. This was the biggest stock-market collapse in U.S. history, before or since. Rich and poor felt its effects. Construction came to a halt. Crop prices fell, causing hardship for farmers. As other nations fell into the same economic hole, demand for U.S. goods dried up. Soon it wasn't just poor Americans eating at soup kitchens, but previously middle-class and wealthier ones, too.

A silver half dollar represented a good sum of money in the 1930s, during the Great Depression. It would have made dinner of ground beef and potatoes for this poor family in Oklahoma.

World War II broke out on September 1, 1939. It would earn the horrific distinction of being the most widespread war in history. More than 100 million people were swept up in its course, with more than 30 countries involved. The totalitarian Nazi Party under Adolf Hitler had taken control of Germany and surrounding countries in a series of campaigns and negotiations, and then launched blitzkrieg—"lightning war"—against Poland. From there the war engulfed Great Britain, France, Italy, and eventually much of the world, including the United States. In the end more than 24 million soldiers were killed on both sides, and 49 million civilians, many of the latter in the Nazis' genocide of Europe's Jews. The United States officially entered the war after Japan attacked the American naval base at Pearl Harbor on December 7, 1941. Industry and government spending in the war effort provided work for many unemployed Americans. As with the Great War a generation earlier, new technologies would change the course of battle, including the first use of computers, jet propulsion, and nuclear power. After a long and horrible conflict the Allied Powers triumphed with the unconditional surrender of Germany on May 8, 1945, followed by the official signing of Japan's surrender on September 2, 1945.

Throughout the war, the Liberty Walking half dollar was America's largest contemporary circulating coin. (The Peace silver dollar was last minted in 1935.) It would be issued for another two years after the war, and then replaced with a new design honoring Benjamin Franklin.

Opposite page: U.S. Army infantrymen in an amphibious landing in the Pacific Theater of Operations, World War II. Above: A half dollar from 1941, the year America entered the war.

LITH.& PUB BY N. CURRICR.   Entered according to Act of Congress in the year 1847 by N.Currier, in the Clerks office of the District Court of the Southern District of New York.   152 NASSAU ST.COR. OF SPRUCE N.Y.

BENJAMIN FRANKLIN.

THE STATESMAN AND PHILOSOPHER.

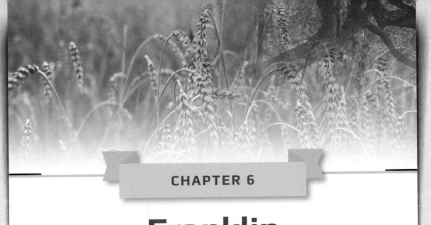

CHAPTER 6

Franklin Half Dollars (1948–1963)

The half dollar of 1948 to 1963 honors one of America's most famous Founding Fathers, Benjamin Franklin—inventor, scientist, writer, politician, and statesman—and illustrates the famous Liberty Bell, a symbol of American freedom. The coin was minted in an era of great change, progress, and challenges.

President Harry S. Truman and British prime minister Winston Churchill.

At the end of World War II, British prime minister Winston Churchill said, "America at this moment stands at the summit of the world." The U.S. economy was finally thriving again, with new cars in production, and plentiful other goods and products. Housing construction ramped up. Beginning in 1946 and continuing through the 1950s the U.S. population expanded rapidly in the so-called Baby Boom. Families regained their confidence in the future, and tens of millions of American babies were born over the ten years following the war.

The 1950s were a decade of prosperity and new technology as well as new consumerism. Television grew into a popular form of entertainment in American homes. *I Love Lucy* debuted in 1951. In 1955 Disneyland opened for the first time in California, and in 1956 Elvis

Presley made his first appearance on live television. The space race began in earnest, with the launch of Sputnik (a Russian satellite) in 1957.

In 1952 Dwight Eisenhower, Supreme Commander of the Allied Expeditionary Forces in Europe during World War II, was elected to succeed Harry Truman as president.

Even with the end of the war and America's return to great prosperity, not everything was rosy. Civil rights were in contention, and international conflicts and tensions simmered. The movement to secure equal rights for minorities continued to battle on, and in 1954 *Brown v. Board of Education* resulted in a landmark Supreme Court ruling that declared it unconstitutional to segregate students by race. The United States was moving, but in fits and starts, in the direction of the full promise embodied in its founding documents.

Princess Elizabeth inherited the throne as queen of Great Britain and its territories in 1952, and was coronated in 1953. This poster advertised the documentary *A Queen is Crowned*, written by English poet and playwright Christopher Fry. Decades later Elizabeth would surpass her great-great-grandmother, Queen Victoria, to become the longest-reigning British monarch.

In the 1930s and early 1940s, U.S. Mint director Nellie Tayloe Ross was interested in honoring Benjamin Franklin on a coin. In 1942 the chief engraver of the Mint, John R. Sinnock, created a motif for a proposed silver half dime, a denomination of coin the United States hadn't used since 1873. His design, which included a portrait of Franklin, wasn't adopted for regular coinage at the time, and the new denomination didn't come about.

John R. Sinnock was the designer of the Franklin half dollar. He died the year before it debuted. His successor as chief engraver, Gilroy Roberts, finished the reverse design after Sinnock's death.

In 1947 Ross directed Sinnock to try his hand at a larger coin, a half dollar, honoring Franklin. Sinnock adapted his design from the earlier half dime, with a portrait of the famous Founding Father on the obverse and a view of the cracked Liberty Bell on the reverse. He had illustrated a similar view of the Liberty Bell on the design used for the 1926 Sesquicentennial commemorative half dollar, inspired by a sketch made by artist John Frederick Lewis.

Sinnock's Liberty Bell graces the reverse of the commemorative half dollar of 1926, which celebrates the sesquicentennial (150th anniversary) of American independence. The Liberty Bell, displayed at Independence National Historical Park in Philadelphia, is a symbol of the nation's freedom. In the 1700s its ringing summoned legislators to session and announced public meetings and proclamations.

In 1948 the new coin was issued. Director Ross gave a speech when the design was unveiled. She said that she'd earlier considered using the cent to honor Franklin, because of his well-known adage, "A penny saved is twopence dear" (translated into more modern English as "A penny saved is a penny earned"). As beloved as Benjamin Franklin is as an American patriot, author, inventor, activist, scientist, and diplomat (among many other roles and accomplishments!), Americans also love Abraham Lincoln, who had been featured on the cent for many years. Replacing him would not have been a popular move. At any rate, Ross reflected in her speech, "The fifty-cent piece, being larger and of silver, lends itself much better to the production of an impressive effect."

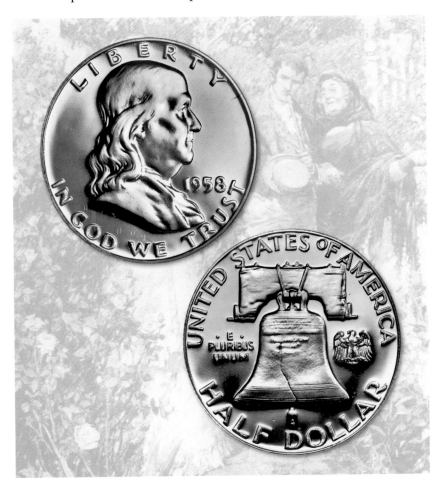

Gilroy Roberts was a Philadelphia-born sculptor, medalist, and postage-stamp designer. He was John Sinnock's principal assistant as a sculptor-engraver at the U.S. Mint starting in 1944, and became chief engraver after Sinnock passed away in 1947. Sinnock hadn't yet finished his design and sculpting of the Franklin half dollar's reverse. Roberts took over the work, helping the coin become a reality.

The main element of the reverse design is the famous Liberty Bell. In 1752 the city of Philadelphia commissioned the bell from a firm in London. It weighs more than 2,000 pounds and measures 12 feet around. Its surface bears the phrase "Proclaim LIBERTY throughout all the land unto all inhabitants thereof." The bell became legendary after a story circulated that it was rung on July 4, 1776, after the Second Continental Congress voted for independence. Although this has been proven untrue, the Liberty Bell still maintains its fame.

You might be wondering about the tiny eagle shown to the right of the Liberty Bell. Roberts inserted the national bird as directed by Mint officials. The Coinage Act of 1873 required an eagle to be used on most U.S. coins with a denomination higher than the dime.

The full history of these fascinating coins is told in *A Guide Book of Franklin and Kennedy Half Dollars*, by Rick Tomaska.

Benjamin Franklin, "The First American," was born in Boston in 1706, making him more than 25 years older than George Washington. He developed into a polymath—a person whose deep expertise covers a significant number of different subjects, and who can draw on that knowledge to solve problems. Other famous polymaths include Leonardo da Vinci and Galileo. Franklin excelled as a political theorist and as a scientist. He made discoveries regarding electricity and the Gulf Stream. He invented the lightning rod, bifocals, swimming fins, the efficient Franklin stove, the glass harmonica, and other useful devices. He created America's postal system, and started its first volunteer fire company and lending library. He was one of the most influential leaders of the American Revolution and continued to serve the newly formed United States until his death in 1790.

The Franklin half dollar was minted from 1948 through the 1950s and into the early 1960s.

On January 20, 1961, John F. Kennedy was inaugurated as president. The charismatic and handsome young chief executive brought confidence to the American people. He proposed a "New Frontier," a program of laws and reforms to explore the "uncharted areas of science and space, unsolved problems of peace and war, unconquered problems of ignorance and prejudice, unanswered questions of poverty and surplus." On the international stage Kennedy navigated the 1962 Cuban Missile Crisis, 13 days of confrontation and tense negotiation with Russia. Many Americans feared a third world war as the United States and Soviet Union were on the verge of launching nuclear attacks.

On November 22, 1963, President Kennedy was assassinated in Dallas, Texas. His death shocked the nation, and hundreds of thousands of Americans attended his funeral in Washington, D.C. To honor the fallen president, Congress quickly authorized a new half dollar featuring his portrait, closing the era of Benjamin Franklin's coin.

Popular president John F. Kennedy was assassinated in 1963.

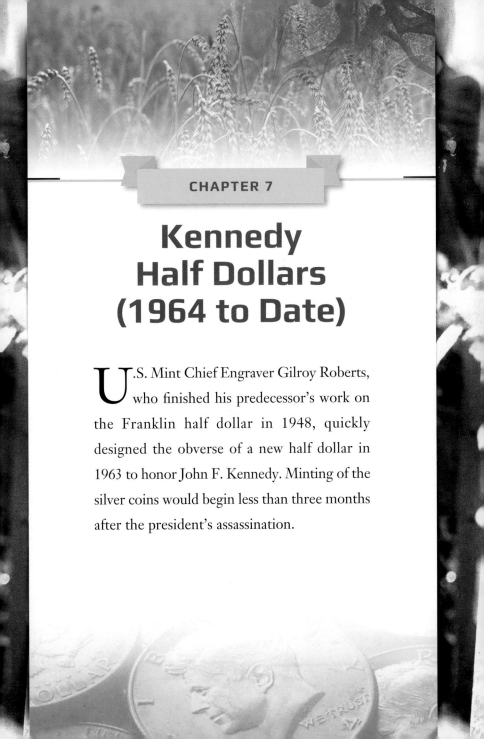

CHAPTER 7

Kennedy Half Dollars (1964 to Date)

U.S. Mint Chief Engraver Gilroy Roberts, who finished his predecessor's work on the Franklin half dollar in 1948, quickly designed the obverse of a new half dollar in 1963 to honor John F. Kennedy. Minting of the silver coins would begin less than three months after the president's assassination.

John Fitzgerald Kennedy was born in 1917 in Brookline, Massachusetts. His father was wealthy businessman Joseph Kennedy, a self-made millionaire and a bank president by the age of 25, a few years before his son was born. Joseph was politically connected and in the late 1930s would serve as U.S. ambassador to the United Kingdom, among other roles and offices. John's mother was Rose Fitzgerald Kennedy, eldest child of the mayor of Boston. She was a dutiful mother and felt fulfilled as a homemaker; a staunch member of Boston's Irish Catholic community, she would be granted the rare honor of being named a papal countess by the Vatican in 1951.

John Kennedy went to school at Harvard. His senior-year thesis, "Appeasement in Munich," would later be published in 1940 as *Why*

The Kennedy family in Hyannis Port, Massachusetts, 1931. John is kneeling in white, background left.

England Slept, a study of the British government's failure to prevent World War II. That same year he joined the U.S. Navy, and in 1943 he commanded patrol torpedo boat *PT-109.* His vessel was rammed by a Japanese destroyer that left it wrecked and burning, and despite his injuries Kennedy led its survivors through unknown waters to safety. Kennedy's war-hero status, his family background, his wholesome look, and his friendly personality made him perfect for politics. After the war he served in the U.S. House of Representatives (1947 to 1953), and then he was elected to the Senate. In 1955 he published a book of biographies, *Profiles in Courage,* that celebrated the integrity of eight brave U.S. senators from John Quincy Adams in the early 1800s to Robert A. Taft, then in office. It won a Pulitzer Prize.

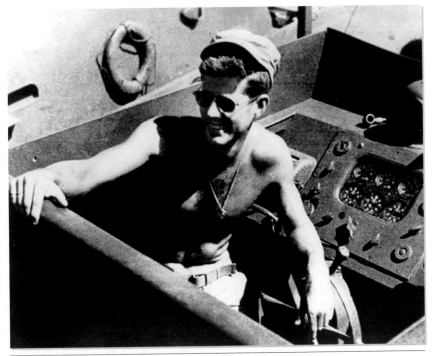

Kennedy in U.S. Navy boat PT-109.

Jack Paar interviewing Senator Kennedy on *The Tonight Show*, 1959.

The president and his family, August 1962, at their summer house in Massachusetts.

In 1959 Kennedy sought the Democratic nomination for president. He campaigned around the country and won several primaries, eventually besting even his most savvy opponent, Texas senator Lyndon B. Johnson. After Kennedy won the nomination he picked Johnson as his running mate.

When critics suggested that Kennedy, a famous Catholic, would listen to the Pope first and the American people second, he replied: "I am not the Catholic candidate for president, I am the Democratic Party candidate for president who also happens to be a Catholic. I do not speak for my church on public matters, and the Church does not speak for me."

The Democratic senator from Massachusetts went on to beat Republican vice president Richard Nixon. At age 43, he was the youngest man elected president in U.S. history. At his inauguration ceremony, January 20, 1961, Kennedy implored his listeners, "Ask not what your country can do for you, ask what you can do for your country," and urged the world to fight tyranny, poverty, disease, and war.

As president Kennedy became known as a family man. His charming wife, Jacqueline "Jackie" Bouvier Kennedy, was one of the most popular First Ladies in American history, and their children Caroline (born 1957) and John Jr. (born 1960) brought playful energy that delighted reporters and the public alike. The family's stylish life earned the Kennedy White House the nickname of "Camelot."

President Kennedy's brothers were also active in government. Robert Kennedy (left) became U.S. attorney general, and Edward "Ted" Kennedy (middle) was a U.S. senator. (August 28, 1963, outside the Oval Office.)

President Kennedy speaking at Rice University, 1962.

President Kennedy formed the Peace Corps, a humanitarian and foreign-relations triumph. His administration worked to try to control global Communism, attempting to overthrow Fidel Castro (supported by the Soviet Union) in Cuba and sending military advisors to South Vietnam (to counter Communist influence in the region). The Soviets were seen as the big threat to America, competing in space exploration, nuclear armament, and other fields. When the USSR shipped ballistic missiles to Cuba in 1962, with the goal of building launch sites so close to the United States, there was a period of anxious negotiation that looked like it was headed toward nuclear war. Finally the Russians backed down and brought the weapons back. This confrontation became known as the Cuban Missile Crisis.

John F. Kennedy worked with Civil Rights leaders, nurtured the U.S. space program, encouraged America's arts, and brought new progressive energy to the national scene. He was widely popular in 1963 as he began laying the groundwork for a run for reelection in 1964. On November 22 he was visiting Dallas to rally Texas Democrats, as part of a multi-state tour. Assassin Lee Harvey Oswald, hiding in a tall building along his motorcade's route, took aim from above and fatally shot Kennedy as he rode by in an open convertible. The entire nation was shocked by the president's unexpected death. Americans everywhere grieved along with his family.

Jackie Kennedy and her children leaving the president's funeral.

Congress authorized a new half dollar to honor President John F. Kennedy just over a month after his assassination. Anticipating congressional action, U.S. Mint director Eva Adams instructed chief engraver Gilroy Roberts to begin work on the coin on November 27, 1963. The president's widow, Jackie Kennedy, preferred the half dollar, not wanting to remove George Washington from the quarter. Roberts had earlier designed Kennedy's official presidential medal, and he used its portrait as the basis for the half dollar's obverse.

For the reverse, sculptor-engraver Frank Gasparro modified the Presidential Seal he had sculpted for an appreciation medal that Kennedy presented to European leaders in the summer of 1963.

The Mint started producing the new coins in January 1964, and they were released to the public beginning that March. There was huge demand for the coins in the United States and around the world, as people wanted a memento of the popular president. Millions of 1964 Kennedy half dollars were saved for this sentimental reason. The Mint originally planned to strike 91 million of the 1964 halves, but the total mintage, after several increases, approached 430 million coins.

Opposite page: The 1964 Kennedy half dollar was minted in Philadelphia (273 million coins, with no mintmark) and in Denver (156 million, each bearing a D mintmark).

A copper-nickel Kennedy half dollar.

The U.S. Mint has produced the Kennedy half dollar ever since it debuted in 1964. The first year's coins were made of 90 percent silver and 10 percent copper. As the price of silver increased through the early 1960s, it became clear that the Mint would begin losing money—it would cost more than 50 cents to strike each coin. The Mint reduced the silver content from 90 percent to 40 percent from 1965 to 1970, then removed silver entirely from circulating coins. Since 1971 half dollars have been made of copper-nickel alloy, except for certain silver and gold pieces minted for collectors.

In the early 1970s the Mint started planning for a new reverse design for the Kennedy half dollar—a temporary change to celebrate the bicentennial of American independence, coming up in 1976. The dollar and quarter dollar coins also received new Bicentennial designs. A competition was held, open to all American sculptors, and for the half dollar Seth G. Huntington's depiction of Independence Hall was

A Bicentennial half dollar.

chosen. This is the historic building in Philadelphia where the Declaration of Independence and the Constitution were discussed and adopted. All Kennedy half dollars minted in 1975 and

A gold 50th Anniversary Kennedy half dollar.

1976 (more than 520 million) had this design, along with the dates 1776–1976. None were dated 1975.

Since 2002, Kennedy half dollars haven't been issued for circulation. The Mint still produces them—and by the millions every year—but the coins are sold directly to the public in sets, rolls, and bags, for higher than face value. They are more like collector coins, rather than everyday pocket change. Silver versions have also been minted for collectors since 1992.

In 2014, to celebrate the 50th anniversary of the Kennedy half dollar, the Mint issued special sets and coins. One was the nation's first gold half dollar, struck with the regular designs but with 3/4 ounce of .999 fine gold.

Kennedy half dollars, and all Kennedy collectibles, are popular today. Two books to help you explore further are Rick Tomaska's *Guide Book of Franklin and Kennedy Half Dollars* and William Rice's *The Kennedy World in Medallic Art: John F. Kennedy and His Family in Medals, Coins, Tokens, and Other Collectibles.*

A bag of 200 2016 Kennedy half dollars, available at www.USMint.gov.

Thomas Ball's statue of George Washington in the Boston Public Garden, Massachusetts; and a 1982 silver commemorative half dollar.

CHAPTER 8

Commemorative Half Dollars (1892 to Date)

The United States has minted special commemorative coins—including many half dollars—for more than 125 years. These coins are rich with history, and each one tells a unique story.

The *Guide Book of United States Coins* describes the history of coins struck in honor of people, places, and events: "Commemorative coins have been popular since the days of the ancient Greeks and Romans. In the beginning they recorded and honored important events and passed along the news of the day. Many modern nations have issued commemorative coins, and they are highly esteemed by collectors."

Your *Search & Save* coin collection can include an example from more than 125 years of commemorative half dollars.

The first U.S. commemorative coins were minted in 1892, to celebrate the World's Columbian Exposition in Chicago, an international extravaganza marking the 400th anniversary of Christopher Columbus's discovery of America. One side shows a profile of Columbus—actually artist Charles Barber's idea of Columbus, since no portraits are known from the explorer's lifetime. The other side features the flagship *Santa Maria* above two hemispheres. These coins (some dated 1892 and some 1893) were sold for $1 each at the Exposition. Five million were minted, which was greater than the demand, and about half of them remained unsold. The Treasury Department later released a large number into circulation to be spent at face value, as if they were regular half dollars. For that reason you will often find these coins in circulated grades, and priced inexpensively.

On the following pages, you'll see a sampling of the dozens of silver and copper-nickel commemorative half dollars minted by the United States since 1892.

Opposite page: The World's Columbian Exposition commemorative half dollar.

A commemorative half dollar was minted in 1918 for the 100th anniversary of Illinois entering the Union as a state. It was the first souvenir coin struck for such a celebration, and others would follow—for the Maine centennial in 1920; the Missouri and Alabama centennials in 1921 (although Alabama actually became a state in 1819, not 1821); California's diamond jubilee (75th anniversary) in 1925; and others.

The Illinois Centennial half dollar shows an unusual view of one of the state's most famous citizens: Abraham Lincoln. What makes it so unusual? Young "Honest Abe" hasn't grown his beard yet! The portrait is based on a statue by artist Andrew O'Connor, located outside the state capitol in Springfield, Illinois.

In 1926 an international fair was held in Philadelphia to celebrate the 150th anniversary of the signing of the Declaration of Independence. Congress authorized a commemorative coin to help raise money to organize the fair. More than one million of the Sesquicentennial of American Independence half dollars were minted— but fewer than 150,000 were sold, at $1 apiece. Most of the rest were melted.

The obverse of the coin shows George Washington, first president of the United States, and Calvin Coolidge, president at the time of the sesquicentennial. This was the first time a living president was portrayed on a U.S. coin.

Designer John R. Sinnock's depiction of the Liberty Bell would later be adapted for use on the Franklin half dollar of 1948 to 1963 (see chapter 6).

The Oregon Trail Memorial half dollar was first minted in 1926, then again in 1928, and in several years from 1933 to 1939. The commemorative program honors the pioneers who moved west, opening the American frontier. Many of them lie buried along the famous 2,000-mile highway of history known as the Oregon Trail. This half dollar's designs show a pioneer family in a Conestoga wagon, heading west into the sunset, and a standing Native American with a bow, his arm outstretched, with a map of the United States in the background.

This was the first commemorative coin to be struck at more than one U.S. Mint facility (Philadelphia, Denver, and San Francisco), and also the first to be struck at the Denver Mint.

Each year from 1946 to 1951, commemorative half dollars were minted to honor a great American educator, author, and presidential advisor: Dr. Booker T. Washington. From the 1890s to 1915 he was the preeminent voice of the African-American community.

Washington was born a slave in 1856, rose to national fame as a political speaker, and built a network of black ministers, educators, businessmen, and other community leaders, along with white supporters, to uplift black Americans through education and other means. Presidents Theodore Roosevelt and William Howard Taft frequently asked Washington for political advice. His tireless work helped lay the foundation for the Civil Rights movement of the 1960s.

No commemorative coins were made from 1955 through 1981. Then, in 1982 the Mint issued a silver half dollar celebrating the 250th anniversary of the birth of George Washington (illustrated on page 80). The coin was very popular, and more than seven million were sold.

The George Washington half dollars were followed by commemoratives for the 1984 Olympic Games, held in Los Angeles . . . then by coins marking the centennial of the Statue of Liberty . . . a silver dollar for the bicentennial of the U.S. Constitution . . . and many others from the 1980s to today. Modern commemorative coins—which include silver dollars and $5 gold coins, in addition to half dollars—have honored American inventors and explorers, branches of the U.S. military, Boy Scouts and Girl Scouts, the U.S. Marshals Service, and other important subjects, continuing the tradition that goes back to 1892.

The Mint has innovated with recent commemoratives such as the 2014 Baseball Hall of Fame coins, struck with curved surfaces to resemble a baseball, and a pink gold coin for breast cancer awareness.

Proposed coin programs are considered by two committees of Congress: the Senate Committee on Banking, Housing, and Urban Affairs; and the House Financial Services Committee. Once a program is approved by Congress, the independent Citizens Coinage Advisory Committee (ccac.gov) and the U.S. Commission of Fine Arts (cfa.gov) advise the secretary of the Treasury on the coins' designs.

Surcharges, or built-in fees, are paid from the sale of each commemorative coin to a beneficiary named by Congress. For example, sales of the 2016 National Park Service 100th Anniversary half dollar benefited the National Park Foundation, a nonprofit charity group.

Collectors buy tens and hundreds of thousands of U.S. commemorative coins every year. Popular reference books that explore each coin in detail include the *Guide Book of United States Coins,* by Q. David Bowers, and the *Encyclopedia of the Commemorative Coins of the United States,* by Anthony J. Swiatek.

CHAPTER 9

Collecting Half Dollars

Your Whitman Search & Save™ coin album is a great way to begin a collection of U.S. half dollars, from the Capped Bust coins of the 1830s to today's Kennedy half dollars, plus commemoratives. You can start with 12 coins of different years, eras, and designs.

Opposite page: President Franklin Roosevelt admiring a 1936 commemorative half dollar minted for the 100th anniversary of Arkansas officially becoming a state. Standing at right is Senator Joseph T. Robinson, whose portrait appears on the coin.

Today it's rare to find a half dollar in pocket change. To collect them, you will have to buy them at a coin shop or at a coin show, through the mail, or someplace else. (Or you might get them as presents from relatives and friends who know you collect coins.) Read books to learn more about your favorite half dollar series. By reading about a coin—how rare it is, how to grade it, how much it's worth in different grades—you will have knowledge for when you start looking to buy.

Go to a coin show and look at every coin you can, from low-grade, worn examples to high-grade coins with bright luster. Ask questions. Soon you'll have a good feel for the coins you want to collect.

For more information on grading, see the *Official American Numismatic Association Grading Standards for United States Coins*, by Kenneth Bressett, or *Grading Coins by Photographs*, by Q. David Bowers.

In Mint State, a half dollar is lustrous and has no wear from circulation, although it might have contact marks from other coins, or light blemishes. Its design details are boldly visible.

In Extremely Fine condition, a coin has less luster and some wear on its high-relief areas— for example, the lines in certain areas of Miss Liberty's skirt.

In Good condition, a half dollar's details are well worn. This coin shows Miss Liberty's head, neck, and arms all flattened together.

The Whitman Classic® Coin Album page in the back of this book has plastic slides that you can insert on each side of the openings. This lets you see both sides of your coins.

Fully insert all the slides to complete the back side of the cardboard album page. Gently push the rounded corner edge of the slide into the opening between the cardboard page and the blue lining material. It can be gently worked into place with a little care.

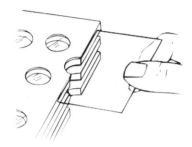

Wear gloves (cotton or latex) when handling valuable coins. Hold your coins by the *edge*. Don't place your thumb or finger on the front or back of the coin, as this can damage it.

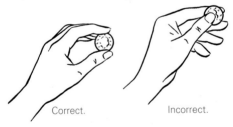

Correct.   Incorrect.

As you collect your coins, set them into the proper openings in your album. Finish up by adding a slide to the front of the page, to hold your coins in place.

These are the coins in your Search & Save™ half dollar collection:

Capped Bust Half Dollar, 1807–1839. You won't find one of these in your pocket change! But you can search for a Capped Bust half dollar at your local coin shop, or in a coin dealer's inventory online. Many dates are affordable for beginning collectors in circulated grades up to Fine and Very Fine. (The opening in your *Search & Save* album is for the larger-diameter varieties of 1807–1836.)

Liberty Seated Half Dollar, 1839–1891. You can buy an attractive Liberty Seated half dollar from a coin dealer. Some dates are more common than others, and therefore more affordable, even in higher circulated grades such as Extremely Fine and About Uncirculated. There were five different varieties minted over the years, with minor design changes in the position of stars, arrows, and legends.

Barber or Liberty Head Half Dollar, 1892–1915. Lower-grade Barber half dollars are common and inexpensive; for a little more money you can collect a nicely detailed circulated example in Fine or better condition.

Liberty Walking Half Dollar, 1916–1947. These beautiful old half dollars are very popular among collectors. The U.S. Mint made millions of them nearly every year from 1916 to 1947, so even Mint State examples are easy to find and affordable.

Franklin Half Dollar, 1948–1963. Franklin half dollars were minted by the tens of millions and you can find a nice example at a coin shop or from a dealer online.

Kennedy Half Dollar, 90 percent silver, 1964. For their first year, these popular coins were made of 90 percent pure silver (and 10 percent copper). Each contains just over 1/3 of an ounce of silver, so even in circulated condition they're worth more than face value. Nice Uncirculated coins are common and inexpensive.

Kennedy Half Dollar, 40 percent silver, 1965–1970. For several years the Kennedy half dollar was made of a combination of metals totaling 40 percent silver. The 1970 coins were issued only in special collector sets, but the earlier dates are more common; all are inexpensive.

Kennedy Half Dollar, Copper-Nickel, 1971 to Date. These are the half dollars most easy to find today. Look for the nicest example possible.

Kennedy Half Dollar, Bicentennial, 1976. Many people saved these special coins honoring the 200th anniversary of American independence. Ask your family members and friends if they have any, or search through bank rolls to find one for face value.

Commemorative Half Dollar, 1892 to Date. A coin dealer can help you select nice examples from the many commemorative half dollars minted since 1892—or a family member might have a recent "commem" to share, or one from years past. Your album page has openings for three of your favorites.

Image credits: Heritage Auctions (ha.com), the world's largest collectibles auctioneer, shared coin images and photographs of historical items. Stack's Bowers Galleries (stacksbowers.com), a leading numismatic firm since 1935, provided coin images. The Library of Congress and the National Archives and Records Administration shared historical images. The United States Mint provided some coin images. Other coin and historical images are from the Whitman Publishing archives. Pg. 11: WestportWiki (modern trucks). Pg. 25: Iconographic Collections (machines). Pg. 29: Nina Aldin Thune (Wise Men). Pg. 32: Brocken Inaglory (lake). Pg. 43: Collection of Dennis Tucker. Pg. 64: Everett Historical (background). Pg. 76: Badr Alzamil. Pg. 77: thatsmymop / Shutterstock.com. Pg. 79: Daniel D Malone (2006 coin). Pg. 90: Miroslav Halama (background). Pg. 96 (coin collectors): VITA PIX; Q. David Bowers (half dollar).

As a publicity stunt, circus owner Fayette "Yankee" Robinson stamped half dollars as "free tickets" to get into his show. The only catch? You had to hand over the "ticket" to get in! Fifty cents was the normal price of admission.